Impunity from Lunacy

Book Two

by

Ellen Marie Blend

Dedication

I am dedicating this second book to my dear friend, Charlie Brown, who devoted much of his life enlightening others about spiritual interactions and spreading words to heal the mind, body and spirit.

Charlie was born in Delta, Alabama, but had roots in Toledo, Ohio, where he ran the Heflin Printing Company, and also The Psychic Eye Newspaper. The newspaper later became Body, Mind & Spirit News, followed by an online publication named Rev. Charlie Brown, after he retired in DeLand, Florida.

I would like to honor Charlie with this second book, as he faithfully printed the many articles that I wrote from 2004 until his death in 2013. This book encompasses my articles published between those years and beyond.

Words of Witicism

For more than twenty years, Ellen Marie Blend has been connected with the spirit world. She receives messages and signs in various ways, but mainly in the mind's eye.

Her writings within are extrapolations of many sorts. She uses this quippy little verse to explain the origins of her work:

Anecdotes and Doze eh? Notes

Anecdote: *A short narrative of an interesting, amusing, or biographical incident.*

Doze: *To sleep lightly; to be in a dull or stupefied condition.*

Eh: *U*sed to ask for confirmation or repetition, or to express inquiry.

Note: To record or preserve in writing.

Her short articles are written after experiencing some noteworthy incidents, either via some sign or

---

Definitions from the Merriam-Webster dictionary.

while in a meditative state, which is sort of like dozing. She sometimes questions the information given her (eh?, an expression more commonly spoken by Canadians) because she has difficulty interpreting the message or cannot believe what she sees.

Other times, because the spirit world understands that she is slow to grasp things, they present the same information to her more than once to make sure that she gets it. She then takes to writing notes of her many experiences until they form a brief narrative.

While some topics are very touching and serious, others may make one raise an eyebrow in question of their validity. Rather than be offended by those who disbelieve her, she chose to present this compilation of articles in a fashion that interjects some cartoon humor and can be enjoyed by all who seek this information.

She chose to present her articles alphabetically rather than in chronological order. Her free verse poetry is noted in italics.

Alphabetical Listing of Articles and Poems

A Gift from Heaven

This may not be the kind of gift you would think came from heaven, but my money angel is very kind to me. You will read more about her in some of the following pages.

I received a generous coupon on line for a popular restaurant that serves very good ribs, and my husband and I like to go there. With that coupon, which was only good on that day, we went to dinner.

As I walked from the car to the front door of the restaurant, I spied a shiny penny on the ground between the two parked cars that I passed through. I stopped to pick it up, and said to my husband, "She's here!" Of course he knew I meant my money angel as he has witnessed her offerings in the past.

We then entered the restaurant and placed our orders. My husband ordered a full slab of ribs, and I ordered a half slab. When the orders were delivered to the table, we both were given half-slab orders, and the side dishes on each plate were incorrect. The waitress took off in a flash before we could catch her.

I tried following her, but she escaped into the kitchen. The manager was at the front desk and saw me look helplessly at the kitchen door. "Can I help you?" he asked.

"I was just trying to catch the waitress as we received the wrong orders."

"I can help you with that," he said, and escorted me back to my table. As he took our orders again, someone from the kitchen brought out the right orders, and our waitress followed right behind.

He kindly directed the waitress to find out who did not get their orders and to take care of it. He also told us to take the ribs off of the plates with the incorrect sides and add them to ours.

By the time we left the restaurant, we actually had a full slab of ribs to take home in our carryout boxes. I thanked my money angel for her generous assistance and her gift from heaven.

A Reminiscent Visit

I had gone to bed, and was in an almost sleep state, when I felt the presence of my late cousin, David, who departed within the last year. I had not felt his being around me prior to this evening.

I telepathically greeted him warmly, and asked if he had seen his mother, my late aunt. I then remembered to ask about his son, as he had passed away a couple of years prior from sleep apnea. I got the feeling that he had seen them both, and others, whom I would also know.

He then began to reminisce of several things that we had experienced together, and showed them to me in my internal vision, or mind's eye. He remembered us as children, and my visits to his home. He also showed me where we played in the playground at the nearby park. Then he reminded me of his fixing my television, and in bringing his family over for dinner.

Another memory he brought to both our minds was of his late son, who loved to fish. My house is located on a lake, and he recalled bringing him over to go fishing while he and I talked at the kitchen table. These were fond memories that he brought to me, and some that I would not have thought about had he not been there to remind me.

A Shared Soul Experience

Several years back I went to see a psychic who used to be my next door neighbor and now lives quite a distance from me. I still consider her a friend and miss that she is not convenient to me. Victoria has many guides, and throughout the years she has been quite accurate with my readings.

This particular day, her reading included that the souls of my former lover and a new man would collide. She also stated that a rekindling of my old flame and myself would not be good for me now.

Sometime later that year I met a new fellow, and our relationship deepened immediately. We were very comfortable together, and many things about his personality reminded me of my past lover.

In time, I found that there were so many things about my new man that were intricately similar to my former lover, that I began to make a list of their likenesses. Soon our entire journey brought the realization of a shared soul experience.

While many questions remained unanswered, my past lover found a way to communicate with me through this new man to complete his karma with me. His soul was able to share space with the new man's soul, and it presented a means for conversation on a higher level.

A Tap on the Shoulder

During the night while I lay sleeping, someone tapped me twice on the shoulder. I woke up. It was not a gentle tap, but I rolled over to see if my husband was trying to wake me. My husband was sound asleep on my other side, and no one else was there.

That morning I was accompanying a couple of girlfriends to an outing which was put on by the husband of one of our deceased friends. "I think it was Gwenn," stated one of my friends. "She knows we are on our way to meet with her husband." I considered that she might be right.

However, earlier that week I received a telephone call from my elderly uncle's daughter letting me know that her father had passed away a couple of days prior. Both my uncle and the daughter lived in other states, and I was told that he would be brought back to his home state, Michigan, for burial next to his deceased wife.

I reflected on this, and then I knew. It was my uncle's strong tap on my shoulder that had awakened me. I also remembered the whoosh of cool air that passed through me just two days before. I hadn't connected who my visitor was at the time, but intuition has told me that he had passed through with a brief visit shortly after his death.

A Touching Send Off

My dearest friend, Gwenn, passed away after a twenty-two year bout with cancer. As her husband so proficiently proclaimed, she went down arduously arguing the point. I've never known anyone with a stronger spirit.

She and I were quite connected here on the Earth plane, so I fully expected communication from her when she passed on. Her last request was to have a memorial service at my home in the backyard.

Her desire was graciously honored with friends and family present. Her closest friends were a group of girls who belonged to a sewing club, and I was part of that club. These girls always managed to pull together in a time of need, and this event was no exception.

To honor Gwenn's wishes, we were to get together in celebration rather than in mourning. We tried to accommodate her desire. At the suggestion of one of the girls, helium balloons were purchased, and we released them in her honor at the end of the memorial service. Each of us wrote a message in our own manner to be attached and sent off with our balloon into the heavens. It was a glorious site.

The Balloons
publicdomainpictures.net

My message read:

To my dearest of friends, and a dear friend to us all, for you always put our lives in your care—and always before yours.

You are an admiration, an inspiration, and an example for us all to strive to be—for your endurance, hardship, bravery, humor, vitality, knowledge and unequivocal spirit.

You have my full love and utmost respect for eternity. May you rest in peace and have everlasting tranquility—now and forever.

That evening, after falling asleep, I was startled by the glare of a picture of fire-red coils in my mind's eye. I was aware that my newly deceased friend was angered about something. I could not imagine what she was upset about since the day went off without a glitch. Even the weather cooperated perfectly. As I asked for more information, she presented a tall black hat.

At first I thought it was a man's top hat, but it wasn't that tall, and it didn't make any sense to me. I was later reminded that her friend, Carol, who resides out of town, did wear a rather tall dark hat that day. I then knew that the message was in regard to her, but could not figure out what could have possibly angered Gwenn as Carol was very touched by her death.

The next day I tried to interpret her message but was at a loss. Shannon, one of the club girls, thought about the undefined message and suggested that our deceased friend was mad that she was unable to see Carol before she died. I thought that she might be on the right track, but the anger still did not fit. I felt that she might have been disappointed, but not angered.

Then it occurred to me what the message was all about. When Carol thought she should come into town, the rest of us thought it would be too hard on Gwenn, and we did not encourage it. The last time Carol visited, it took a toll on our ill friend where she never regained her strength.

While none of us ever told Carol not to come, we must have influenced her, and our deceased friend was angry. We were looking out for what we felt was in her best interest, so now all we can offer are our individual apologies.

The next evening another message came from her. This time I saw Gwenn's face clearly. She wore a light red candy-striped blouse that I recognized, and she was looking up into the sky. Again, failing to interpret the information given me, I consulted Shannon. Very quickly, she said, "The balloons. She was acknowledging the balloons."

Printed in Fate Magazine

Alien Encounter

For those of you who enjoy reading about aliens, I had a mind's eye experience from a young female alien. I questioned whether it could have been a dream, but I have recently had others visit me. My visitor was gentle in her movements, and she tried to explain the eight levels of her existence.

On a recent evening, I began to see faces of people that I didn't know. Then a flash of something went by, and I thought, "That looked like aliens." It was as though I had called out to the passersby, as two alien visitors came back into view.

One was clearer than the other, and again, female. The heads were alien shaped and bodies were green, as is so often represented in pictures. I found it strange that they should appear along with human faces from planet Earth, but it was more confirmation that they do exist.

Because they seemed to gaze in at me, I became alarmed that they had come to take me from my earthly existence. I was concerned about being abducted, and quickly sent them away. They seemed to understand my fear and have not returned.

Always Money

From the time I was in my late teens, I was totally self-sufficient. I had a secure, well-paying job, and was able to take care of all of my personal expenses. In my early twenties, I moved out on my own, still well able to pay my own way for everything.

I knew little of Guardian Angels, but I found that money was always coming to me. Raises would show up in my pay, checks would come in the mail, and I always had ample funds to cover my needs. I was aware that some form of money seemed to appear periodically. It was never an exorbitant amount, but enough that I was always comfortable.

Today, much later in my years, the pay check is not there, and the checks do not show up in the mail. However, my son, who has struggled financially for many years, is now receiving benefits similar to my past luxury. Perhaps my money angel has taken to watch over him.

Angel Healer

I had been dealing with a cold for several weeks. When I realized that it had been a full month, I began to search for additional means to help boost my immune system.

Apparently my concerns were heard, as I had an angelic visitor appear in my mind's eye as I lay quietly in bed. I was ready for sleep, but saw an emerald green angel wing cover my entire view with a feather-like appearance. I recognized it as an angel wing at once, having had other angel visitors cover my internal vision with their lovely wings.

The next day I referred to my book of angels, and I learned that the color green was from one of the Powers, whose purpose is to heal. She had kindly heard my silent request for help and had appeared.

Angel Wings of Snow

As a child, I often made angel wings in the snow by lying down and raising my arms in an upward movement, and then putting them down again at my sides. It was always great fun to see the angel outline that I made in the snow.

Today, as an adult, I have more profound angel visions. As I lay in bed, waiting for sleep, my guide, who may be an angel, shows me many visuals. Perhaps it is a face or place that I don't recognize, or a scene that I cannot identify. Sometimes it is just a confirmation that my guide knows what I am experiencing.

For instance, after a day of much snowfall that covered the ground with mounds more than a foot deep, I was shown a scene of buildings, with patches of snow stuck all over them. I saw this scene through a blinding snow, just as it had been that day.

The buildings soon disappeared in this internal vision. Picture a window pane with large snowflakes stuck all over the window like patches of frost. That is about what I saw, only the snowflakes were pure white feathers of angel wings that covered my entire vision.

I can only assume that an angel wanted to let me know that she was there to give me comfort and protection.

Baby Talk

For some reason, I have a guide who is very interested in new babies coming into the family. Having four daughters-in-law in their child-bearing years has given way to being informed about three of the new births without even asking.

When my son's wife, Sherrie, was expecting, I suddenly saw handwriting with the word "boy" enlarged on my mind's visual screen, so I knew I would be getting a grandson. Since the couple did not want to know the gender of their child in advance, I certainly didn't tell them.

A year or so later, I was given a visual of a baby girl, with a wide smile and big cheeks. The baby was wrapped in a green blanket. My husband's middle daughter, Anna, soon announced that she was expecting, but I was confused because Sherrie loved the color green. She decorated her entire house in shades of green, including the grandson's room.

When no announcement came from her regarding being in a motherly way, I was left to wonder. Then one day, Anna came over with her two boys, and one of them had a green blanket. "Anna," I said, "that's the color green!" Anna delivered a baby girl with the widest smile, and beautiful cheeks. I had no doubt then what baby I had seen.

Now the youngest daughter, Terry, is expecting. She and her husband know that they are having a girl. She asked me if I had any visions of her or her baby. Soon after, I saw a baby girl wrapped tightly in a pink blanket. Close by was a symbolic vision of water spurting out. I interpreted that to mean that Terry's water would break early.

When I told her what I had seen, she asked me when the baby would come. I told her I hadn't been given that information, but after that vision I had the number 3 come to me. I confessed that I didn't know if it was a psychic message or if I had just thought of the number.

Since Terry has had medical complications, she and her doctor agreed that she should go to the hospital shortly before her due date and have the baby induced. However, when she went for her next doctor's appointment, upon examination the doctor told her that she had dilated to 3 centimeters. He also told her that she had lost 3 pounds, finding that information equally worthy of my message.

When in the hospital, her husband sent me a text message saying that she was still dilated to 3 centimeters and at 3:03 p.m. they broke her water in order to start the process.

California Retreat

Cassie, a friend of mine, has been able to share some spiritual experiences with me. At one time, she wrote of an experience that she had while living in California. This is what she said:

"Living in California brought me to the awareness of reincarnation and a completely different spiritual understanding. Many of my personal psychic experiences have occurred during my dreams. The most intense moments I have ever had took place while on a retreat in Big Sur, which is off the Pacific Coast Highway, just south of Carmel.

"Big Sur is so mystical, and the scenery is breathtaking! It's one of my favorite places. My very dear friend, Cheryl, was with me. We were attending an Art and Spirit weekend when a flood of 'other world' experiences began to occur. It was incredible and also very difficult to articulate. Art was the medium that we utilized to express these experiences. Cheryl is a massage therapist and often channels during a session. She is quite remarkable."

I have since met Cheryl and can appreciate her fine talents.

Charlie's Vase

As I prepared my previous book for publication, I wondered if my late friend, Charlie, knew that I had dedicated that book to him. The thought lingered a while, and then I dismissed it.

Charlie had published countless articles that I wrote on paranormal experiences in his publications of *Psychic Eye, Body, Mind and Spirit News*, and then *Musings*, which was a separate section of his website *Rev. Charlie Brown*.

Charlie's printing business and psychic newspapers were in Toledo, Ohio. He later gave his current newspaper to a member of his staff and moved to Florida to live with his brother. He then started an on-line publication *Rev. Charlie Brown*.

While still in Toledo, Charlie had a party for his printing and newspaper staff, and I was invited. He gave out many gifts, and for me, a yellow vase covered with angels.

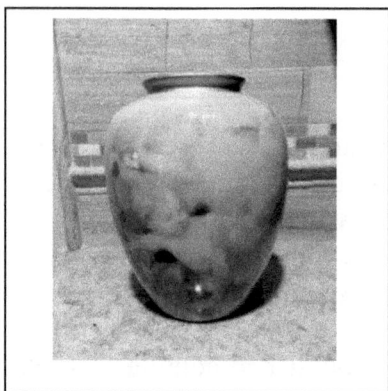

Charlie's Vase

One day as I was perusing a local thrift store, I saw the identical vase to the one Charlie had given me. Now I had my sign. Charlie knew that I had dedicated my book to him.

Colorful Messages

My friend, Katie, is both intelligent and spiritual. She has psychic ability, but her talents are different from mine. She does not communicate directly with the spirit world as I have learned to do. So, having a few dilemmas in her life, she asked me if I could get some answers for her. I said I would try, which for me meant to be alone at night and to meditate.

The first evening, in a meditative state, I asked her first question. She had arthroscopic knee surgery several months earlier and wanted to know if a new procedure called platelet rich plasma would be good for her. No one came from the spirit world to answer the question, and I drifted off to sleep.

Another evening, I could sense the activity of spirits around me and asked again. I immediately received a page of Arabic writing, which of course I could not read. Was my guide from Egypt or somewhere in the Middle East? Or was the message advocating against introducing a foreign, extraneous procedure?

بِسْمِ اللَّهِ الرَّحْمَٰنِ الرَّحِيمِ ۝
الْحَمْدُ لِلَّهِ رَبِّ الْعَالَمِينَ ۝ الرَّحْمَٰنِ الرَّحِيمِ ۝
مَالِكِ يَوْمِ الدِّينِ ۝ إِيَّاكَ نَعْبُدُ وَإِيَّاكَ
نَسْتَعِينُ ۝ اهْدِنَا الصِّرَاطَ الْمُسْتَقِيمَ ۝
صِرَاطَ الَّذِينَ أَنْعَمْتَ عَلَيْهِمْ غَيْرِ الْمَغْضُوبِ
عَلَيْهِمْ وَلَا الضَّالِّينَ ۝

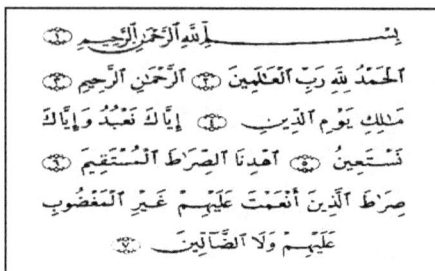

Arabic Writing

Then, additional writing appeared diagonally across the page in red. I tried to rationalize if I was being told that the procedure would involve red blood, but my feeling was that the red was a sign that the procedure would not do her good.

Since I had the attention of a guide, I went on to the second question. Katie had been on a hormone therapy and was having some undesirable side effects. She stopped using the hormone patch and felt much better.

She wanted to know if she could continue to go without the therapy. This time I saw the same page with diagonal writing in blue, which then changed to green. I understood this to be that it would be good for her to

30

stop the therapy for a short time, but that she would need it again.

The third question of concern was regarding Katie's late mother. Her mother had passed away a year ago, but she never sensed that she was around her. After her father's passing, she continually felt his presence, but she wondered why her mother did not visit.

Katie and her mom had a strained relationship a few years prior to her passing, but they mended their misgivings a year before her death and enjoyed one another's company. When I asked why her mother had not come around, the writing that appeared was now in green. I also got the following infused message. Her mom was around but was keeping enough of a distance to protect her emotionally.

Dreams of Past-Life Homes

My cousin's wife has had many recurring dreams, each focusing on a portion of homes that she believes are from a past life.

She recalls seeing an older home, probably in Europe, that had a winding stairway that led to a second floor. On that floor was a long narrow hallway that had closets with shelves in them. In one closet there were gowns...old gowns like the ladies wore in the 1800s. Some of the shelves had linens on them, many of which had monograms, but she could never make out the lettering or design.

A second house was a newer home, like a brick ranch; however, when she would go upstairs to the attic, there was an entirely different house. The upstairs had rooms that contained absolutely beautiful furniture. She remembered that there were four bedrooms that were connected with small rooms in between. This would be very bizarre by today's home standards. Again, the linens and furniture were of very high quality.

Then there was a third house, and she only seemed to remember the upstairs again. As she walked up the staircase there were about six or seven doors. Each door contained a room, such as a library, a den, an office, etc. Again, the furnishings had very elegant styling.

She has had the same dream many times, and is of the belief that they are from one of her past lives. She says, "Since we are immortal we could have experienced many past lives." She has never seen the outside of any these houses except for the one that looks more like her own present-day ranch. She must have had one or more very aristocratic lives by the size of the homes and the furnishings they contained.

Duncan's Sister

My friend Duncan's parents lived in different countries. His father lived in England, and his mother, divorced from his father many years ago, lived in Australia. Duncan generally alternated visiting England one year and Australia the next to see his family.

Because of this separation of parents, he had a brother in England and another brother and sister in Australia that he wished to visit each time he traveled to their country. His sister, however, had a falling out with the mother and has disappeared from the family. Duncan has tried to find her many times and finally asked me if I could tell him where she was.

The first thought that came to mind was Chelsea. Before I answered him, I wanted to be sure that there was a Chelsea, Australia. I found that it is a suburb of Melbourne, Victoria, south of where his mother resides and about 45 minutes away.

This is what else I was able to tell him:

Your sister is in a house. There is a man there. He looks like a nice man. He has dark hair, a full face but not round, and a mustache. I think he smokes. He smiles at her.

Your sister is very busy. There is an ornate object in the house.

I picture a tub of some sort beneath the object like a wash tub. My thought is that the object may be an antique that she is cleaning. It looks more like metal than wood, but I cannot be sure. I think it is a music stand.

I don't believe Duncan ever traveled to Chelsea to find his sister, but I gave him as much information as I could.

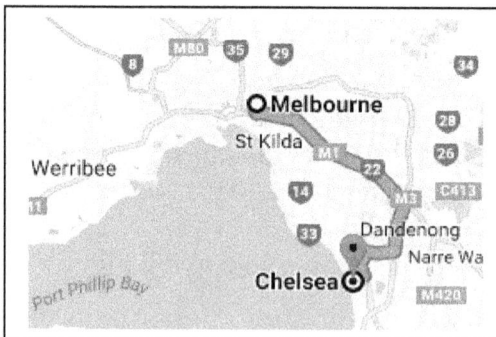

Edna

My husband and I had gone to a Paranormal Festival. I was a vendor, selling my books, but was able to participate in the conference to hear many of the speakers. During the happy hour the first evening, we met some very nice people and were able to converse with them throughout the next couple of days.

While attending one of the talks the first evening, I sat next to a young woman, a medium, who was waiting for her husband. We shared a few stories, and the one I mentioned was about my money angel who has been with me probably throughout my life. I mentioned that she sees that I always have just enough money.

The next morning, that couple invited us to join them at their table for breakfast. They were an interesting and fun couple, and we were pleased to be in their company. We learned that her husband had become very spiritual since being guided through his wife's abilities of psychic channeling.

At breakfast, the wife asked me if I had been calling out to her or thinking about her during the night. I replied that I had not, as I slept very soundly. "Oh," she said. "Well someone kept me up during the night. I'll have to ask around and find out who knows Edna."

"Edna!" I exclaimed. "That's my money angel!"

Some time ago I had read something about how to ask your angel for his or her name. I did the exercise, and the name Edna came through ever so lightly. Then the article instructed to do the exercise again to confirm the name, but I could never get confirmation.

Apparently, Edna was unable to get that information to me, but used my new medium friend to do so.

"She just confirmed her name for me!" I said. "Thank you for delivering her message!"

Electrical Chaos

I seem to have an unidentified entity around who is intrigued with what can be accomplished with my electrical devices. Since I have physically seen my own little Gremlin, and a somewhat helpful fairy has placed herself visibly on my computer screen, I know that they are both around. However, since I cannot see the current intruder, I don't know who to hold responsible.

Whoever it is has managed to tamper with my television, my computer, my car, a floor lamp, and possibly my furnace. The furnace appeared to have a short in the wiring, and the floor lamp decides when it will operate and not. The car battery gets worn down because an interior light that I didn't use has stayed on in the car or the lighted trunk has popped open whether I used it or not.

Other strange things have happened with the television. All of the people on the screen turned white for just an instant, then returned to their normal coloring; sometimes the entire screen flashes all white for just an instant. Yesterday, the gentleman broadcasting the news was put into a freeze frame for more than a solid minute before he could continue the news.

Then, as I was writing this article with the use of my computer, some of the consonants appeared double, and I had to remove them. Also, in an earlier writing, my computer spell check alerted me that I had spelled "frenzy" incorrectly. The correct spelling, it told me, was "f-r-i-e-n-z-y"; so, with some doubt, I changed it. When I tried to verify the word by its meaning, I was again corrected to spell the word "f-r-e-n-z-y" as I had spelled it in the first place. I elected to change the word altogether. I had a similar problem with the word chaos, but I stuck with using its original spelling.

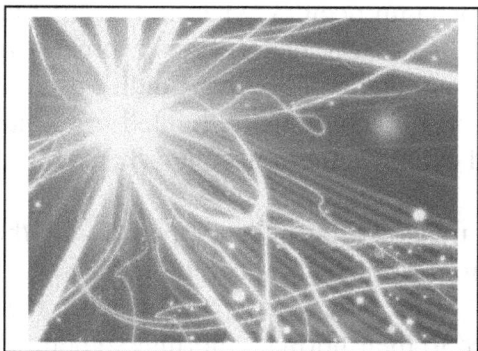

Electrical Chaos
Dmitriy Chistoprudov

As with other psychic phenomena, when I tried to repeat the steps for confirmation of what just happened, the bazaar occurrences could not be replicated. When I told my son that I seemed to have an electrical gremlin who was messing with my computer, he said "Mom, everyone does!"

Eye Chart

Using eye drops before going to bed seems to be a difficult task for me to remember. I often forget and find my eyes dry and scratchy in the morning.

One night after having gone to bed, my spirit guide flashed me an eye chart. Not getting the message, I thought, "What was that all about?" and drifted off to sleep.

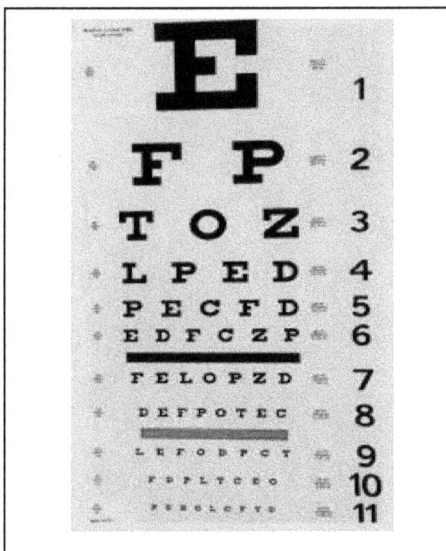

Sometime later, I awakened and remembered seeing the eye chart and figured out that I had been reminded to use the eye drops.

Another night, just settling into bed, I jumped up with a start. "What's the matter?" my husband asked.

"I have to go use the eye drops, or my spirit guide will be showing me an eye chart!"

Fate's Hand

As a New Age and Spiritual author, I find that "Sometimes you need God's intervention to make things happen." I had seen a former friend twice recently in a local establishment. Our friendship had been severed over a legal business issue and we had not spoken for over ten years. When we found each other in close proximity of one another, we were each too afraid to speak to one another, yet recognized the opportunity. I was afraid he would make an embarrassing scene if I approached him.

God intervened. Months later, God placed me in a line to purchase tickets for an event where I saw some people that I knew ahead of me. I left my present company to go say hello, to find my former friend in line behind them. I was introduced to the friend they had accompanying them, and then to that friend's date, who was my former estranged friend.

I could only say, "Oh, I know you," and we each shook hands to get reacquainted. His broad smile told me that past issues had been put aside. Now, should we meet again, we will be able to converse comfortably with one another.

Forgive Me

I had attended a holistic fair and rented space to display and sell my books. Late one afternoon, an intuitive psychic came in by the name of Sharon, and she had a table directly across from mine. Before she even set up, she came over to me and put her hand on one of my books. She asked if that was okay, and I told her yes. She then began to tell me some things about my family.

She seemed to instantly identify with me, and after a couple of days working across from her, I felt we had become great friends. One of the things she told me was that there was something on the tip of my mother's tongue that she wanted to say before she died, but didn't get the chance.

I immediately thought she meant my grandmother, as she had made a profound statement to my mother from her death bed. So, I interjected, "Yes, that was my grandmother. When my mother said to her, 'Don't worry, I'll take care of Dad,' my grandmother said, 'He's not your father.'" That, of course, was shattering and I thought that was the information that the psychic was talking about.

Months later, I saw Sharon at another event. We renewed our friendship with a warm greeting, and before the evening was out, I told her that I had regretted cutting her short with the information she had given me. I told her that I had probably been mistaken with my comment back to her.

When we had a few moments to ourselves, she asked me what that was. I repeated her earlier statement and my error. "Oh yes," she commented. After a brief hesitation, she said, "Forgive me. Your mother wanted to say, 'Forgive me.' It wasn't that she didn't love you; she didn't know how to love."

She then asked if that made sense to me. It did. She also said, "Toward the end of her life, while on oxygen and fading in and out of consciousness, she left. Wherever she went, she came back feeling the love and wanted to ask for your forgiveness."

Forward View

I rarely remember my dreams, but this time I did. A former girlfriend, Joanie, and I were very close at one time. We worked together, shopped together, and vacationed together. We were both single at the time. Years passed, and our lives separated. By then, both Joanie and I had left the company we had worked for. Joanie took another job at a shopping mall, and we seldom saw each other.

I had heard that a former gentleman co-worker that we both knew had seen her working at the mall, and had recently lost his wife. She and the man we worked with began dating, and then traveling together. She became so consumed in the relationship that her friends never saw her anymore.

I thought of her often, as I had always been quite fond of her. She appeared in my dream, just as attractive as she had always been. She had aged, of course, as we both did over the years. As I watched her in my dream, her face became older still. The vision of her continually aged, and her cheeks became gaunt, but she retained her attractiveness just the same.

Now, I wonder. Was the dream presentation
a view of her life in the more distant future?

Funeral Mass Visitation

My friend Katie's mom had just passed away, and she and her mom had suffered a poor relationship for four years since her father's death. They had only resumed their friendship over the last year, giving Katie much needed peace and enjoyment. Upon her mom's death, she says she feels cheated for the years they did not maintain a mother and daughter relationship. She misses the years that they lost.

Since she and I are able to converse on the spiritual happenings in each of our lives, during our visit together she told me that her mom was very clairvoyant and that is probably where she gets the gift. Katie is also religious, but that does not inhibit her from seeing many apparitions of those she loves.

In fact, Katie was so inundated with spiritual interaction at the time of her mother's death, she said, "I asked my spirit guides not to visit me on the night before my mom's funeral as I needed to get a good night's rest. There was so much activity for the few nights previous that I didn't get much sleep."

"At the funeral," she told me, "my late father, grandmother, grandfather, uncle, aunt and a lot of people I didn't know showed up at the back of the alter during mass. There was such a loving crowd. Also, my dad was there at the gravesite to greet my mom's casket. It was quite amazing and very comforting."

Glowing Aura

My husband and I had been invited to celebrate our relatively close birthdays with his sister at her home. She had lost her husband slightly more than a year previous, and was learning to entertain others in her home by herself.

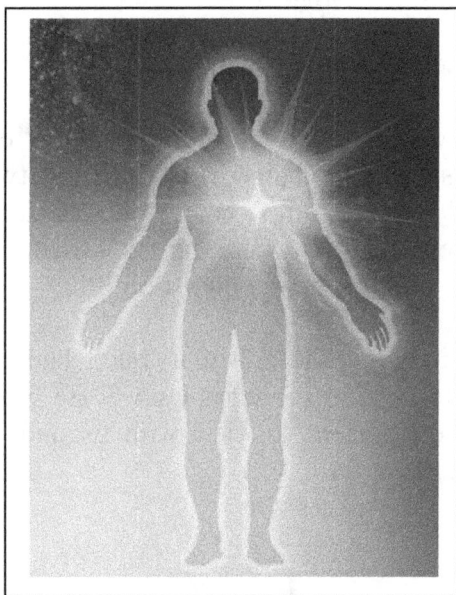

Glowing Aura
Rossie Nikolova

We visited in the living room, and my husband and I sat in chairs in front of a picture window. His sister sat in a bright colored chair against the opposite wall. She often spoke of her late husband, John, in her conversation, but has adjusted to her new life as well as can be expected.

As she spoke, I noted a bright, glowing light about six inches wide surrounding the bright colored chair against the wall. I said nothing about it, but after leaving, I mentioned it to my husband.

"That was John's chair," he said. "He always sat in that chair. In fact, the last two times I visited him before he became bedridden, that is where he sat when we visited. You just saw John's aura!"

Indeed it was quite spiritual, but I had no other explanation for what I saw. He must have been present to visit with us and to comfort his wife.

Grey Shadows

I had fallen asleep on the couch one evening and awakened to see dark shadows of people standing in my living room. There were three, and I squinted my eyes to see them more clearly--or as clearly as one can see shadows. I closed my eyes and then opened them wide to be sure I was actually seeing them.

They were definitely of solid substance and without facial characteristics. I would describe them as a dark, thick, smoky grey and without facial detail. One was tall and the other two were short. The tall one seemed to be standing near a tower rack of CDs in my living room. The other two were near the wall unit where my television sits. The television was not on. I acknowledged that they were there, but did not speak to them.

My friend, Gwenn, is very intuitive. When I mentioned to her that I had seen them, I explained that one was tall and the other two short, as if they were in a sitting position. "Maybe one was standing at the end of a bar and the other two were sitting at the bar," she said.

55

I could just imagine seeing the tall one leaning against the bar rail, with one leg crossed in front of the other, while talking with the two at the bar.

"I didn't say anything to them," I said.

"What makes you think they could hear you, anyway?" she countered. "Maybe they couldn't see or hear you."

Hair Dryer

Janie and I had become friends for only a few years when she became terribly ill. She was diagnosed with stage 4 lung cancer.

She and I seemed to understand each other quite well, and I was probably the only one who agreed with her decision not to have chemotherapy. She felt that her immune system was not that good to begin with and that she would not survive the treatments.

As it turned out, she lived more than a year longer than the doctors predicted if she were to have had the treatments. I think that she appreciated my support, and her other friends told me that she had always been very fond of me.

Her closer friends knew of her desire to be laid out in the back porch sunroom of her home. In fact, she had new door walls installed so that visitors could easily enter and leave through those doors without tracking through her home.

After she passed, her brother took over her arrangements and was in agreement with the in-home viewing. However, a last minute change of heart, causing much confusion to visiting friends and relatives, was to have her body moved to the funeral home that made the arrangements.

Having learned this information rather late myself, I hurried to get ready and to make it to the funeral home before other guests arrived. I had washed my hair and was trying to use my hair dryer, but it wouldn't work. I pushed a couple of different button selections, but none of them worked even though it worked perfectly a few days earlier.

I scurried around to find my husband's hair dryer, but tried mine again. I even used the reset button on the wall receptacle to see if that was the problem. I settled on using my husband's dryer and went on to the funeral home.

The next day I tried the hair dryer again, giving it one more chance before throwing it away. It worked. I guess my friend, Janie, was letting me know that she was not happy with the arrangements having been changed. The hair dryer has worked perfectly ever since.

Hand of Divorce

For many months I vacillated on whether or not to get a divorce from my first husband. There were things in the marriage that I didn't feel I could live with, and I was quite unhappy. Yet, because I still did love my husband and the fact that he was so good to me, I vacillated.

I finally went to a marriage counselor to discuss my concerns. I attended several sessions, with the counselor helping me sort through my reasons for unhappiness. Finally, in what ended up being my last session, he asked me this question.

"Do you think if you waited that your husband would change?"

I thought about it for only a moment, and said "No." I got up from my chair, extended my hand in a farewell greeting, and said goodbye.

The next day I filed for divorce. After that moment of truth, I felt the big hand of divorce push me through the steps that I needed to take in order to leave him.

There was no more consternation, no more questioning in my mind, and no stopping the propulsion that I felt. I was physically being pushed through the process right to the end.

That push was an unseen guide. My guide must have been waiting for me to finally decide, and was there to see me through.

Handicapped

In my relaxed and meditative state, many people would come to see me before I would go to sleep at night. I did not know them. They peered over me much like doctors and attendants looking down at a patient on an operating table. Some were elderly, many were not, and occasionally even an infant would present himself or herself.

I inquired about this with Cassie's intuitive friend, Cheryl, the massage therapist. She explained that these individuals needed to draw upon my energy to stay on the Earth plain with their loved ones. I thought about this and began to feel used. I closed them out until they no longer appeared.

I discussed this feeling later with Cassie and explained that I felt guilty for not helping. She said that I didn't have to help them, but suggested that I could set limits.

"You could tell them that you would accept those of great need on one particular night of the week," she said. I thought about this and considered it to be a viable solution. I still liked helping people, even those on the other side, but I didn't want to feel used.

Upon retiring that evening, many people again came to visit. However, each was handicapped or deformed in some manner. They had shown up because of my mental agreement to help them.

Healing

Without having a plan, I became immersed in psychic phenomena from having numerous experiences. I began writing about them to document and share my learned knowledge.

In addition, I became interested in faith or psychic healing. I was only at the state of having an interest about this technique when the spirit world directed me to learn more.

My friend, Gwenn, had breast cancer that had spread to her hip. She was now walking with a slight limp as it had affected her spine as well. She asked me to move my hand across the area where she felt the pain to see if I could feel anything. I did, and succinctly felt the heat energy in my hand as I passed the cancerous areas.

"I can't feel that," she exclaimed. "You should look further into that as you probably have a healing touch."

I asked the spirit world for direction during a meditative state. My face became very warm, without cause, as I ran my hand over it. I was being told that I should indeed follow that path.

Higher Self

There are many opinions of what the higher self is, but from what I understand, the higher self is actually you. You on the Earth plane is just a projection of the consciousness of your higher self, who holds the blueprint of your life plan that you agreed to before your incarnation.

In my case, I find that my higher self watches over me very carefully. Many times when I close my eyes to rest, mostly on a sunny day, she is able to peer in at me. When my eyes are closed, I actually see her looking back at me. I see every mark and imperfection in my face, on hers, and she even blinks when I blink. It's like looking in a mirror.

It is thought that through your connection with your metaphysical self, you can manifest your desired future, and create your own reality.

His Heart is with Me

A loved one of many years ago was a spiritual man, long before I had taken that path. One day he said to me, "Call me Caleb."

"Caleb," I said as a statement more than a question.

"Yes, Caleb."

I had no idea what he meant, and a search of the biblical Caleb left me without an explanation as to what he was trying to convey.

We separated, and years have passed. I have since married, and only recently saw a picture of him wearing a wedding band.

In the early years of our separation, we were able to communicate telepathically. We experienced a strong and undying love, even though separated. At one point of receiving his telepathic messages, I was told "Go on with my life," and in another, "I'll always be with you."

Now, I have been receiving signs that are to relate a message to me. He has recognized that I am aware that he remarried. We are obviously still connected through spirit.

I also keep seeing the name "Caleb" in several places. It keeps reappearing, and is certainly not a common name in today's world.

I again looked up the name "Caleb" on the Internet, and find that in Hebrew, "kal" means whole, or all of, and "leb" means heart. It is an expression of faith, devotion, and whole heartedness.

Now that I have received the message, I will probably not see the name again. In spirit, he is letting me know that he is still wholly devoted, and his heart is with me.

How Doest Thou Cast A Shadow?

My eyes are shut,
my head is resting on a pillow,
and I am ready
to drift off to sleep.

Suddenly, I sense a shadow
cross in front of me, and
I open my eyes to find
there is no one there.

"No one has been there
except you,"
I say to the spirit world.
"I cannot see you,
but I know that you are
there."

I then wonder,
if I cannot see you,
"How doest thou cast a
shadow?"

I Saw You

My husband is a retired teacher. He often enjoys sharing teaching experiences with his daughter, Anna, who also became a teacher. When they talk, they are able to share stories of their classrooms, teaching methods, and some of their good and difficult students.

To add to my husband's enjoyment, his daughter occasionally invites him to her classroom to talk to her students. He is quite proud of her accomplishments as a teacher. He visited her classroom just before Halloween where she was teaching Spanish.

The next morning, I made a comment to my husband. "I saw you and Anna at school," I remarked. I often saw visions in my mind's eye when going to bed.

"You did?" my husband questioned.

"Yes. Last evening, when I went to bed. You were in the classroom with Anna."

Disbelieving, he asked "Did Anna write on the board?"

"Yes," I said.

"What did you see?" he asked.

"Oh, a couple of big, overlaying circles, sort of like a pumpkin."

"Do you know what a Venn Diagram is?" he asked.

"No," I confessed.

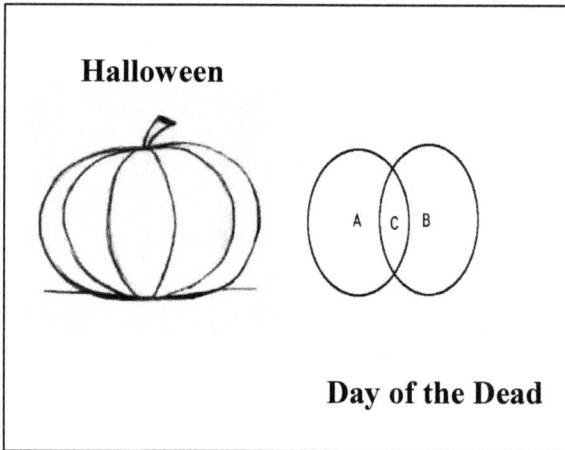

Halloween

A C B

Day of the Dead

"It's two circles that overlap. Students offer their ideas about two things and discuss their similarities and differences. The teacher writes the ideas in one or the other circles, and the diagram shows where the two are alike in the overlapped portion. She was talking about the similarities and differences between Halloween and the Spanish Day of the Dead."

He was amazed to find that I was able to see this information. So was I.

"You were on the left and Anna was on the right as you faced the blackboard."

"Yes, you're right," he said.

It is not often that I am presented with this type of information, but it was fun to report this to him and find that what I saw was correct.

If I Were a Rich Man

My husband was always trying to win money. He didn't want the money for himself, or even for us. He donated to charities frequently and abundantly, even though he would later say, "I could sure use that money now." Even so, he continually gave away many sums of money to those in need. He always wanted money to help others and to give it to the church.

Perhaps one of my guides had the tune played for me, but having recently heard the well-known song from Fiddler on the Roof, "If I Were a Rich Man," I found that the song continued to replay itself in my mind. The tune stayed with me for a long time, and I noticed myself hearing it throughout the day.

It played in my mind so regularly that I wanted to think that money was coming my husband's way. He had been entering a lot of sweepstakes, but I knew that the "if" in the song was just as dubious as intended. If he were a rich man, he could give all his money away.

In Shame

From experience, I knew when I saw a picture in the newspaper of a gal that looked like my deceased friend, Celia, that she was trying to make contact with me. That was a way for spirits to let you know they were around.

Celia was one who never took care of her health. She ate whatever she wanted, and only what she wanted, because that is what she liked. She also tended to drink alcohol too often, and carried much more weight than she should. In fact, her excess weight finally prevented her from getting around, and her knees gave out. She needed surgery, and finally, with diabetes and sores that wouldn't heal, her life ended prematurely.

A few days passed before I was able to take the time to meditate after getting into bed. I asked God for his white light of protection, and received it right away. Then, I asked for Celia, and she came forth quickly. I saw a couple of different views, one perhaps when she was in better health, and then as she was at the end of her life.

I was so happy to see her. I asked, "Celia, how are you? Are you doing okay? Are you happy?"

It wasn't until I asked if she was happy that I got a response. She immediately dropped her head, as if in shame. I assumed that she was letting me know that she was ashamed of the lack of care that she had given herself and realized that it cut her life short. With that, she disappeared from view.

Interim Death

A friend of mine told me that her brother-in-law had endured three heart attacks, one right after the other. He told her that during the third attack, he knew that he had died. This is what he said:

> I saw my wife and others that I had known in this lifetime. I had been regretful, because I had not been kind to my wife prior to her dying with cancer. I immediately told her that I was sorry, and that I wanted to stay there with her.

> "I know you are, but you can't stay," she said. "You have to go back. Our daughter, who was born with Down syndrome, has lived a long life for her condition. You are going to have to make some very big decisions about her in the near future, and you have to be there to take care of her."

> "But I want to stay here with you," he protested.

"I know," she said, "but you have to go back."

In that instant, I was whisked back into my body and found the medical staff working on me.

He felt gratified that he had been forgiven, but now faces the upcoming decisions that he will have to make regarding his daughter.

It's a Boy

My son and his wife had announced that they were going to have a baby. I was very excited for them, as they had married later in life, and it was a first marriage for both of them.

I asked them if they wanted a girl or boy. They both agreed that they didn't care. In fact, they didn't want to know what they were having until the baby was born.

As time went on, and having the normal tests along the way, they still took precautions not to find out the gender of the baby.

I certainly didn't care either. In fact, I thought it rather old fashioned, and sweet, that they wanted it to be a total surprise.

One of my friends asked the mother-to-be how she would know how to decorate the baby's room.

"Green," she said. Green was her favorite color, and now also her married name.

One night when I lay sleeping, I was awakened to see a scroll of yellowed parchment paper with script handwriting across the page. I couldn't read it, but my guide kindly enlarged one of the words so that I couldn't miss it. "Boy," it said, as plain as could be.

Now I had to refrain from telling them and everyone else I knew that "It's a Boy!"

It's Elementary

I once met a gentleman while attending a networking meeting. I was single at the time, and this gentleman was showing a keen interest in me. I could see that he was married by the ring on his finger, but the attention was flattering just the same.

Though he inferred that an affair could be had, I welcomed his friendship with set limitations. We have since become good friends, and now I am married.

However, during this period of enchantment, I questioned my guides as to what his discontentment might be in his marriage. It did not appear that he had any intention of leaving his wife, even though he claimed that she did not support him in his interests.

One night I asked the spirit world for answers. I was shown a schoolroom and blackboard with elementary lessons written on the board.

It's Elementary

Oh, I surmised. Men have often been bored with their marriages and have sought outside female attention. "It's Elementary;" a basic need for love and nurturing.

Just Ask Your Angel

My friend, Linda, was married to a very good man. His only flaw seemed to be that he drank to excess when having a good time with family or friends. It was his nature to be excessive with many things, but any over indulgence of alcohol was a big problem to Linda.

When she confided in me how much it bothered her, I suggested that she ask her angel for help. "Angel's are very willing to be of assistance," I said. "They just need to be asked."

Linda prayed to her angel for help. The next day brought a surprise. When getting together with friends, Linda noticed that her husband drank a limited amount. It appeared that watching his weight became important, and he was careful not to consume too many calories.

Linda smiled as she realized that her angel had come to her rescue. She thanked her kindly for her brilliant assistance and hoped that this good fortune would last.

Looking Out After You

My husband, his two sisters, and I entertained five out-of-town family members for the weekend. One of the sisters never married, and the other lost her husband a couple of years ago.

My husband and I welcomed our guests Friday afternoon, and later had a nice dinner for them. Rachel, the sister who lost her husband, provided Saturday's backyard fun and a dinner that evening, while the other sister, Julie, took everyone to breakfast on Sunday morning before our guests departed.

On Saturday evening, after dinner, there was much discussion as to who was going to church in the morning, or should the out-of-town guests leave early in the morning and go to church in their home town in the evening. If they went to mass here, what mass should they go to, who was driving who, and so on.

After the decisions were all made, Rachel was to be dropped off by Julie, who would go directly to the restaurant to arrange seating for all of us. Rachel was to get a ride from church to breakfast with our guests who had gone to church in their vehicle.

When we gathered in the restaurant for breakfast, Rachel, who was to catch the ride, was missing. There was so much confusion over the various plans the evening before, that those riding in the same car did not remember that they were to bring her to the restaurant. In fact, as it turned out, they never saw Rachel at the church at all.

Rachel soon realized that she was in trouble, without a ride, and mentioned it to one of the lingering parishioners. The gentleman assured her that it would be no trouble to drop her off as he was going in that direction anyway.

She explained her theory to the nice gentleman of what had probably happened, and they had interesting conversation on their way to the restaurant. Nearing their destination, she asked him what his name was. "John," he said, and that brought tears to Rachel's eyes. "That was my late husband's name," she said.

"Well," said John, "he's looking out after you."

Love on the Other Side

Once when I had been fantasizing about a loving kiss between a couple on a television program, a handsome gentleman came to me later in the evening during a meditative state. In full embrace, I was given the most romantic kiss.

I recognized myself, but I was not who I am now. I can only surmise that he and I had an endearing love sometime in a past life.

I wondered if I would ever see him again, and to my surprise he has appeared twice since then. In each of those times, he has only peered in at me, but it is somewhat comforting to know that someone on the other side cares deeply enough to watch over me.

Male Singers

I was recovering from a bout with the flu and had fallen asleep on the couch. It was the second day of my illness, and except for still being tired, I was feeling pretty good. As I awakened, I heard the voices of angels singing. I smiled at the recognition of this, but couldn't immediately place why they sounded different from the first angels I had heard some time ago.

After I replayed their sounds in my head, I realized that the first angels I heard sing a few months ago were female, and these voices were definitely male.

I tried to describe the sounds to my husband, telling him that it was similar to what I had heard before, a beautiful harmonious sound.

"Was it more like a hum?" he asked.

"Yes, that may be a word for it," I said, "but I'm not really sure there's an accurate word to describe their beautiful harmony."

May I Interrupt this Broadcast?

Before retiring for the night, I flicked on the television and climbed into bed. I needed to slow my busy mind down with some entertaining program after a hard day's work.

As my mind drifted, I began to think of the many unanswered questions I had about things going on in my life. I knew that I needed to meditate on them for guidance.

With the noise of the television as interference, I said to myself, "Well I can't ask now; the spirit world can't make it through all of this clatter."

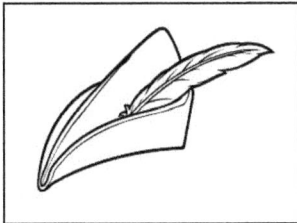

Archer's Hat

Then a young man appeared wearing an archer's hat and slowly made his way across the corner of my television screen. He tipped his hat and gave me a wink as he passed, letting me know that he could indeed interrupt the broadcast.

Meteor Shower

I had just read the paper and found that a meteor shower was going to be visible over the next three or four nights, probably between two and three o'clock in the morning. It would have to be very dark, and in an area without city lights, in order to see the shower or shooting stars.

"Slim chance of that happening," I said to myself. "I won't be getting up to see it."

That night when I went to bed and closed my eyes, my spirit guide kindly made a beautiful meteor shower visible to me in my psychic vision.

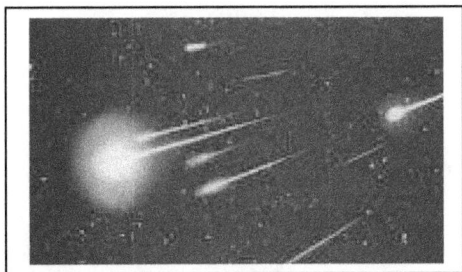

Meteor Shower

I smiled, thanked my guide, and proceeded to see whatever other visions were brought to me before drifting off to sleep.

Misdirected

Sometimes it is difficult to understand why you are strongly sent in one direction, and then it doesn't work out. I will tell you of a set of circumstances that happened to me.

My son was about to lose his home through bankruptcy from being in business with his father. He was looking for a smaller house to buy or rent and found one of interest in a nearby city. He took me out to see the house, which was on a beautiful canal; in fact, three canals converged into one, making a crystal clear lake off the back of this property.

Across from that body of water was a large house that piqued my interest, and it was for sale. We drove back to the main road and down another to see that house. It turned out to be a very large boat house, with outdated living quarters, and was part of the property across the street. The main house on that parcel was fairly new and was 3,000 square feet.

With the living quarters in the boat house and the house across the street, my son and I considered that we could both contribute to make the payment. I could not afford the property on my own, but together it was doable. I put an offer in on the house. My son made plans for renovation of the boat house property for his living quarters.

We were both excited about the properties, but I soon became ill. I felt depressed, and worried about the additional half-hour drive away from everything that I did. My son never shared his true feelings with me, but I sensed something didn't feel right to him either.

Fortunately, another buyer came along and made an offer on the property. His offer did not have a contingency while mine did. I could have gotten a bridge loan until my house sold, but I didn't feel comfortable about doing that and it probably would have been more than I could afford. I wanted out.

The new offer released me from the deal and I got my deposit back. My son and I were both relieved, and we each managed to stay in our own homes. I believe the exercise was to prove to my son that I was there to help and support him, and it has been a solid relationship ever since.

Money Angel

My husband and I were on vacation and decided to stop at a store. As we were on our way from the car to the store, I found two pennies on the ground in the parking lot.

I remarked to my husband, "There has to be one more; my money angel wouldn't give me just two pennies. There has to be three." I don't know how I knew this.

After our shopping and finding what we needed, we were at the checkout counter. The sales girl was ringing up the order when I found another penny at the end of the counter beyond where she was standing.

"There it is," I said to my husband. "She just gave me the third penny."

Later that day we went for a walk along the beach. There were benches to sit on near the water, and we stopped to rest. My husband found nine pennies under the bench.

"My money angel wouldn't give us nine pennies," I said. "There have to be more."

A little while later, we moved to another bench out of the sun. Again, my husband looked around. This time he found lots of pennies over by a tree. I don't recall just how many, but I think my money angel just wanted to prove that she indeed was there and was capable of providing plenty of pennies to prove her existence.

"That's more like it," I said. I know my money angel. I will never be rich, but I always know that she is watching over me.

Mother Mary

As I lay in bed and drift off to sleep, I am often visited by those on the other side. Sometimes I see just a glimpse of someone peering in on me, but this time it was Mother Mary. She held her cape across her face, just under her nose, but her eyes were clear and round as she looked upon me.

"Mother Mary?" I asked. "Is that you? How do I know that's you?"

Then, she backed away, and showed herself holding baby Jesus. Then I knew for sure that it was Mother Mary, and that she had come to look in upon me.

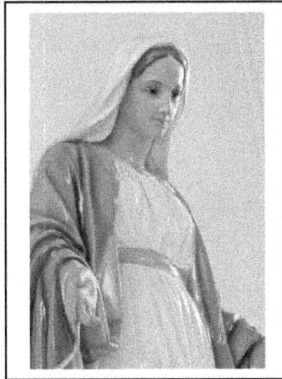

Mother Mary

My Golden Friend

I had grown accustomed to frequent visits from St. Michael. I was comforted by the glow of his golden light.

Several months passed, and he had not appeared. I was afraid that I had lost my connection to the spirit world, as other spirits had not appeared either.

Then one evening, when I was washing my hands, bright golden bars of light appeared in the sink and across my hands. "St. Michael, you're back," I exclaimed.

Now, as before, when I sit reading in the evening, St. Michael spreads his golden light across the words on the page as I read. My golden friend is with me.

Negative People

My dear friend, Gwenn, had cancer for the second time, and I was taking her to the hospital for chemotherapy treatments.

During the first visit, I saw dark images of people come forth, one at a time, against the off-white wall. They appeared as a negative image with dark faces and white eyes, noses and lips. When we were by ourselves in the room, I told Gwenn of their presence and that she was not there alone. She was comforted by this knowledge.

Negative People
Dtvector

By the second treatment, I realized that all of those people were "negative energy" – a sign I had not readily understood. With all of the ill people in that chemotherapy area, they attracted much negative energy. I mentally told them to leave.

The next visit produced only one negative image, a male, who appeared in a circle of white light. I did not trust this "negative" person either, and also sent him away. When he re-appeared, I sent him away again. I had recalled some scripture that said that even Satan disguised himself as an angel of light.

Soon a totally white image of a lady appeared and stayed at Gwenn's side during the entire treatment. She had no facial features, but I trusted her. I later learned that this white image was an angel, called a "white lighter," and was there to help heal my friend.

Printed in Fate Magazine

News Flash

My husband and I were sitting at the kitchen table when the light above us began flickering. "It's going to burn out," he said.

"No it isn't," I said. "It does this once in a while. Maybe it's a short in a wire or something."

"I don't know," my husband said, as he glanced at the light in the stove clock. There have been times when the stove light would dim when the overhead kitchen light flickered.

"Well, I bought a replacement bulb the last time it flickered like this, but that was months ago and it still hasn't burned out. I wonder what spirits are in the house," I said.

"There aren't any spirits here," he huffed.

The light continued to flash on and off, driving each of us a little crazy. I had to admit it was more than normal and was lasting a very long time. "How annoying," I said. "Do you want me to turn the light off?"

Before he could answer, the telephone rang. It was one of my girlfriends from my sewing club. She called with the shocking news that the husband of one of the club members had passed away that morning.

The kitchen light has burned steadily from that moment on.

That flickering light going off and on was actually a news flash, I surmised. The spirit was warning me of the upcoming news.

News Flash

Numbers, Numbers, Numbers

Many years ago I went to see a tarot card reader who was from out of town and visiting a friend. She was very good, and her readings helped to pay for her trip.

Lots of people were invited to have their cards read, and a large waiting room in a basement of a home housed many people who sat around and chatted with one another. A few alcoholic beverages were served as we waited, and the time seemed to take forever for my turn to be called.

Eventually I was invited to go to a private room to have my cards read. The lady was quite informative, and gave me much needed information about my daughter and other family members. Throughout the reading she kept repeating, "Numbers, numbers, numbers."

"Do you work with numbers?" she asked.

"No, not really," I replied. "Maybe some, but not a lot."

"I don't know what they mean, but they keep coming to me."

A year passed, and the psychic lady was again visiting from out of town. I went for a second reading.

"Numbers, numbers, numbers," she said.

"You said that last time I saw you," I countered.

"Well, I see them again. I'm just telling you what I see, but I don't know what they mean. Do you?"

"No, I don't. I don't have any more numbers in my life now than I did a year ago."

Years later, I have remarried, and my husband is a retired school teacher. Every day of his life he calls his bank and verifies his checking account. He also keeps a calendar, and each day he crosses out a day and counts down to a specific event, even if it is the number of days until Spring.

Additionally, many days he draws lines on a piece of paper and figures out how much money he has. He then itemizes what he needs or wants to spend, adds up the column and subtracts it from his starting balance. Numbers, numbers, numbers.

Do you suppose that psychic could see that far into the future, or her guide, or mine, knew my destiny?

Paying Respects

While a few of my family members can attest to having seen an apparition either of someone they knew, or not, my son, Doug, now has experienced seeing one in human form.

He had attended a funeral on his dad's side of the family. It was for Gerald, an elderly gentleman that had married Aunt Millie very late in life. I'm sure both were over seventy-five years of age when they married, and had enjoyed ten to fifteen years together.

Gerald passed away first. Doug attended the funeral with other family members. At the funeral, standing around the casket at the gravesite, two or more people heard Gerald talking.

When the small service was completed, the family members returned to their vehicles. Doug stayed back to see the casket lowered into the ground, and as he turned around, he saw Gerald walking away.

"He was just checking things out," my friend, Gwenn, stated.

A year later, Aunt Millie took leave. The night prior to her death, Doug had strong and fond memories of her come to mind. He reflected on her always saying, "Stop by and see me." She always said that whenever they were together. The following day he learned that she had passed on.

"She was just saying goodbye to everyone," Gwenn again gave comment.

"That's not the first time that has happened to me when someone dies," said Doug. I'll be thinking strongly about someone and learn the next day that they have passed on.

Pillow Talk

I sit on my couch
with the television on
and my thoughts wander.
I pick up a magazine from the coffee
table and peruse its contents.

I sit perfectly still and know not
where my thoughts have drifted,
when the pillow on my couch
tosses itself onto the floor,
bouncing until it comes to rest.

I search my conscience to see
if my thoughts had traveled
to some baseless place.

I cannot remember where
my thoughts had been;
they were now fully concentrated
on that pillow on the floor.

I was cautioned and reminded
that I was somewhere
that I should not have been.

I had just been given warning.
The spirit world is near and
I am aware of its presence
and message.

Prognosis

Janie, a dear friend of mine, called an ambulance to take her to the hospital emergency room two days in a row. She experienced uncontrollable and frightening spasms in her left arm.

By the time she arrived at the hospital the first day, the spasm had subsided, but the hospital took x-rays of her arm and chest and sent her home. The following day the symptoms re-appeared, and she again went to the emergency room. This time she was admitted.

In order for Janie to leave her home, she had to call upon a neighbor to stay with her mom as she was her mom's full-time caregiver. Mom suffered from beginning stages of Alzheimer's and had recently had a shunt placed in her brain to control Non-Performing Hydrocephalous (NPH), or water accumulation on the brain. This disease also causes Alzheimer's symptoms.

I thought Janie's spasms were caused from having too much stress on her in taking care of her mom. However, on the second day of her hospital stay, she received devastating news that she had lung cancer.

Each day brought more distressing news. The cancer was stage 4, the most serious. Tests revealed that it had spread to her brain, causing the spasms, and possibly into her liver. She took the news with a most positive attitude.

Later she told me, "When I was told that I had cancer, it was almost a relief; I am so tired."

In the next few days she arranged for her mom to be placed into a home for care, something she would not ever have considered previously. She had no choice, and no family able to help her.

How she managed this in her state of mind, I have no comprehension. She found an ad in a church paper for an opening in a home right near her house. It was truly a blessing arranged from above. She thought it would be so convenient to get to her mom frequently with it being located so close to her home.

A few months previous, she had bought a newer, used, four-door car. It was to be used to take her mom shopping and to her appointments. Within a few days after arranging for the home for her mom's stay, Janie found out that with a brain tumor and spasms, she should not drive any longer.

The home that Janie arranged for her mom did not usually accept Alzheimer's patients, but they agreed to take her mom on a trial basis under Janie's trying and serious circumstances.

Her mom was such a delightful and loving person that it worked out well; in fact, the owners of the home claimed that it was such a pleasure to have her bright smile and pleasant disposition each day.

I took Janie for consultation at several hospitals, in and out of state, with each doctor telling her that she had between three weeks to a year to live, with or without treatment.

Her acceptance and demeanor stayed firm and pleasant—she was remarkably calm and unwavering. No one could understand how she could stay so cheerful. She was never a drain on anyone who took care of her.

Her statement was that she was looking at this as a new journey, and that we all had to leave here at some time. I could see that her faith would carry her through.

While she needed transportation for everything that she did, several friends stepped forward to assist her. No one could have been more gracious than she, and I never once heard her complain about her circumstances. She only stated how blessed she was to have such loving friends.

One evening, one of my other friends was going to see a psychic reader for direction in her life. I asked her to call me with the results of her reading.

When she called, she delivered information that the reader had given her for me, but particularly pertaining to my friend, Janie. The report was that I should take care of myself because I was a healer and needed my energy; I should also pursue healing further. While this was very welcomed information, her next message was more astonishing.

She said that Janie's soul was in the process of making a decision on whether to stay or go. If she decided to go, she would go very quickly. If she decided to stay, she would get help; her prognosis was not cast in stone. I would help her either way.

I thought that the reading was profound, and I delivered this information to Janie. She was equally moved and most anxious to share it with her elderly aunt and uncle as well as a few friends. She asked me if it would be alright to do this, but I had no reason for her not to do so.

Janie decided to seek out treatment at an out-of-state alternative cancer center. Still, each new piece of information was more devastating. Her blood work was found to have extremely high counts for cancer, meaning that it was throughout her whole body. She would still have to wait for further results called "markers," which had been sent across the country for analysis and would take about ten days.

In the meantime, radiation treatments were given for the brain tumor to reduce its size and hopefully prevent a stroke. Other treatment for the lung cancer might be chemotherapy and specific enzymes given intravenously or by infusion.

Miraculously, these "markers" were returned with a result of negative. Her type of cancer was treatable, and she would take a new drug for the lung cancer that had recently been approved by the Federal Drug Administration.

This cancer had an 80% success rate, and she would not need chemotherapy. Remission was expected within three to four months. The term "cured" is reserved for those persons who are cancer-free for five or more years.

When I spoke to her on the telephone and she gave me this wonderful news, she said that she would be returning home on Wednesday. She was so elated with this prognosis, and so was I.

I said to her, "So, you decided to stay!"

"No," she said. "I'm coming home Wednesday."

"That's not what I meant. Your soul decided to stay. If you decided to stay, you would get help. I'm so glad you're going to be around."

Ralph

I was in search of past-life information and learned about a channeler who did readings. The information she would give would be conveyed from a spirit guide, either one of hers or mine. I went to see her.

One of my guides came forth. "Do you know Ralph?" the channeler asked. I replied that I did not. She told me that he had red hair and was a jolly man.

I was told in this reading that Ralph had decided to watch over the living of my life. He was there to see that I took every opportunity to live my life fully and to not miss things. He pointed out that I needed to learn to trust in others and to let go of my guarded self.

Later, he appeared in my mental vision as an adult from the 15th century, and again as a small child on a hillside in what I believe was Switzerland. And he appeared again on a plane, sitting across the aisle from me and he engaged in conversation with my friend who had traveled with me.

It wasn't until much later that I realized that "Yes, I did know Ralph," I had come across him in different ways, but I really didn't know anything about him.

Do you know your spirit guide?

Recognizing the Messenger

I sat working next to an acquaintance as we tended a table to check members in for a musical event. I've spoken to Eleanor several times and have always enjoyed her conversation. She told me that she has cancer and is getting chemotheraphy.

She then proceeded to tell me about a strange lady that had come to her house one day, knocking on her front door. She was not expected, and said she was just in the neighborhood and thought she'd stop by. Her conversation was friendly and lighthearted, but Eleanor did not invite her in.

Another day the lady showed up again, without invitation, and this time Eleanor let her in. They discussed many things and found that they had much in common and a lot of stories to share.

Eleanor still found her to be strange, appearing out of nowhere.

They discussed going downtown and taking in an art exhibit, which was of interest to both of them. The lady suggested they go on Friday, and Eleanor agreed that Friday might be a good day. However, on Friday, Eleanor was very sick from the chemotheraphy and was not at all able to go when the lady showed up at her door.

After the woman left, Eleanor began to think that maybe this lady was a messenger from above, sent to bring her some cheer during her health situation. When she felt better later that afternoon, she called her new friend and apologized for not being able to go. She told her, "Don't give up on me; I'd like to be your friend."

Many of us have on-Earth guides that give us comfort and direction, but we're not aware of their purpose in our lives. I told her that she was probably right about the woman, and was glad that she recognized the spiritual experience.

Red is the Color

Recently, when I was going through my closet, I pulled out a purple skirt on which I had sewn some beautiful red ribbon flowers. I use to wear that skirt with a red hat at the Red Hat ladies' events, but I still find the skirt attractive today.

When I went to bed that evening, the usual busyness of active spirits began to appear in my mind's eye. I could see my mother in the upper right-hand corner of my visual screen, and she was wearing a purple dress with a red hat. The Red Hat ladies did not exist when she was alive, but she was obviously admiring the striking appearance of the red and purple colors.

As I watched, she modeled for me, and did some stunning poses I had never seen her do. She also scattered tiny red lights all over my visual screen. Usually, after having such a visitation, the vision is quickly gone. This time my mother lingered around me, because the red lights continued to appear for some time as I tried to get some restful sleep.

Red Wallet

I love lots of colors, but like many consumers, I am attracted to the color red. I also love to dress completely color coordinated. I usually buy a red wallet, simply because I'm attracted to the color.

When my daughter was attending classes at church, a lady in her class stated, "Carry a red wallet and you'll always have money."

"So that's why you always buy a red wallet," my daughter said. "You always seem to have money!"

Yes, I did always have money. There was always money coming to me, as if seen to it by a Guardian Angel. I always had just enough to take care of the things that I needed.

It was much later that I learned that I really did have a money angel watching over me.

Ringin' in the Information

For centuries, the bell has been used to get the attention of the seeker—the cow bell, the dinner bell, and the doorbell. To get my attention, the spirit world has used a similar approach. The ringing of a bell tells me that a little fairy is trying to make contact with me.

One night before going to sleep, I asked for some assistance. Before anyone came forth, I drifted off to sleep. Hours later, I was awakened by the ringing of a bell.

A little fairy came forth in my mind's eye to give me answers to my quest. "I'm surprised no one has told you," said the female guide. However, I didn't know the fairy's real purpose, so didn't understand her message.

It wasn't until much later that I learned that fairies were concerned with the Earth and nature, and I should concentrate on all things natural.

Rose of Sharon

My dear deceased friend, Celia, always gave me excess Hosta plants from her yard when they became overgrown. She would invite me over to dig one or two up, which I did, and put them in a pale of water so that they would be easier to separate later.

I would cover my trunk with plastic so that I could get them home without making too much of a mess in my car. I planted them at home, and they caught life beautifully again in my yard.

One particular day, she had me walk to the back of her yard where a neighbor's Rose of Sharon bush had proliferated wildly, and little shoots had worked their way through the fence into her yard. "Here," Celia said, "take a couple of these, too. You'll like them when they flower."

I planted them in my yard, too, but they did not take. They would grow for a short time, but then they would wilt and die.

Another friend, Janie, who had become ill with cancer, also offered me Lily of the Valley from her yard. She knew that I liked the plant, and often told me to bring a shovel over and dig some of them up to take home.

I never seemed to have the time. I was either taking Janie to a doctor appointment or helping her shop for groceries, and digging up Lily of the Valley did not seem a priority.

Now both lady friends are deceased. To my surprise, a Rose of Sharon has shot up right in the front of my house, and it is now as tall and strong as it can be. I thought maybe I had acquired a self-starter from my neighbor's Rose of Sharon bush, but her blooms are pink and mine are white.

Then, I noticed Lily of the Valley plants shooting up in my flower garden. I have never planted any on my property, and none of my neighbors have them. So, that tells me that both of my friends found a way to gift me with flowers long after their passing.

She's Incredible

When I think back over the years of how many things I thought about wanting, and the number of things that were put in front of me, I say, "She's incredible!" I now realize that my angel has delivered them before my very eyes. I'll just mention a few, but they continually happen.

I had just put in a new bathtub and tile in my bathroom. I wanted a small towel rack, within the tub area, to hang my washcloth to dry. I rigged up a short expandable curtain rod, and painted it gold. I then glued small hooks to the tile to hold the rod, as I didn't want to drill holes in new tile. It worked.

However, when perusing through odds and ends in a thrift store, I found just the kind of rod with hooks that I had imagined wanting. It was quite similar to what I had created. I didn't buy it because I would have had to remove the hooks that I had already glued, and would have had to re-glue the new set anyway. I have never seen another one since.

Another time, I wanted a very small magazine rack to attach to the wall, the size to hold a Reader's Digest, Prevention Magazine, or Guidepost. Just after that thought, one appeared in a store in a color that was perfect for where I wanted to place it. She delivered again, and I also have never seen another one since.

Also, when updating my bedspread with one of another color, I wanted to replace an unmatched afghan. I saw one in a store, on clearance, at an affordable price. I didn't buy it as I didn't want to spend the money. I've regretted it ever since, as I realized that my money angel put it there for me to purchase, and I didn't do it.

She's also the angel who puts pennies in front of me to find, just so I know that she's around. Since I hadn't seen any change for me lately, I mentally asked if she was there.

A short time later, when walking by my bedroom closet, there was a penny on the floor with a hole drilled in it. I smiled, as I realized she wanted me to carry it with me so that I would know that she was always with me.

Soul Transfer

Having personally experienced the transfer of one soul to another being, I authored a book of this topic called "Conversing on a Higher Level." I now find that I am witness to my dear, deceased friend Gwenn, temporarily relaying her messages through my husband. It is a transfer of information from her soul to his. I'm sure that she wants to let me know that she is near.

Gwenn hated humidity. She sensed it in the air much sooner than anyone else I had ever known. "Humidity, humidity, humidity." That's all I heard as soon as the summer season arrived.

Since her parting, and the arrival of my husband, the complaints of humidity are still near. He appears to feel it as sorely as she, and I can't help but think that she is sending me a sign that she is around me through his similar expression.

Other actions and comments also strengthen my belief, but there is one that truly gave me confirmation. The St. Clair River is about a 40 minute drive from my home. Long ago, Gwenn referred to this river's name as the

St. Mary's River, which begins much further north, from Lake Superior.

One day, referring to the St. Clair River, my husband called it the St. Mary's River. Then I knew that Gwenn was sending me a strong enough sign to recognize her continued presence in my life. She had always been around to guide me, and she wanted me to know that she is still with me.

Speaking Out of Place

I was at a psychic event with several readers and a few vendors, like myself. I was sharing a table with another author who had written a book channeled from Mother Mary. Her book was much about Revelations.

I asked her about the channeling, and how she got the information. She explained that she heard Mother Mary's voice, just as plain as she and I had been talking. She also said that she was given explicit directions to be ready to take notes at a specific time each morning, and if she was late, Mother Mary was displeased.

As we sat through the afternoon, talking about many spiritual events, she shared a personal story about one of her deceased acquaintances.

Right after she told me, the books she had on display suddenly fell over and landed on the floor. It was like an invisible hand brushed them off the table. Mine still stood upright and were on the same table with hers.

"Oh," she said, with a questioning look. "Maybe I wasn't supposed to tell you that!"

Special Assignment

Saint Germain and I have been friends for some time now. His visits to me spiritually are frequent, and he is usually accompanied by St. Michael. Each were kind enough to present themselves to me individually in full body view, so that I would understand who they were. I had been confused as to their identities.

Since then, I am able to recognize their presence by their vibrant color, in spirit. St. Germain is always that violet flame, and St. Michael, usually appearing first, is a bright golden yellow.

Having missed their appearance in recent weeks, I specifically inquired as to where St. Germain was, as he seems to be the dominant figure. No answer was forthcoming the first few times I inquired.

Then, St. Germain appeared, but not in his usual form. He came alone, and it looked as though he had been bound in white rope. He didn't stay long, but I was left to wonder what that message was to mean.

Was he being detained? Was he "tied up," so to speak? I couldn't imagine someone from the spirit world being punished, but he did look somewhat imprisoned. I'd rather believe that St. Germain is on special assignment and not able to visit at this time.

Spiritual Tears

When my dear friend, Gwenn, was alive, we use to go out on my boat. She loved the water and took great pleasure in fishing, even if she didn't catch any fish. She had her own gear and knew how to bait her hook and remove the fish from the line gracefully. When she did catch fish, she always released them back into the water. It was the relaxation and sport of fishing that she liked.

We would spend a good part of the day on the water, and while she never objected when I was ready to come home, I could tell that she would spend more time out there if I was willing.

One day, after winterizing my boat for me, my son suggested that I should think about selling it. He felt that it was getting older, and that I might want to look for a newer boat before I found myself with expensive repairs.

I followed his direction and sold the boat, but did not replace it. For a few days after the sale took place, I would see drops of water running down my bathroom mirror.

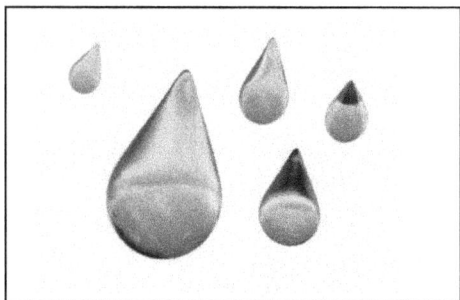

Spiritual Tears

I was puzzled at first. I couldn't understand where the water drops were coming from. Then I realized, they were spiritual tears. Gwenn was letting me know that she was sad that I sold the boat.

Spiritual Visitation

A gentleman friend of sometime past claimed to have had a spiritual visitation.

When he came over, he told me that he had taken a walk in the woods that morning, and that God had come to see him. I asked him what happened, and this is what he said.

"God visited me today. 'Are you ready to take me?' I asked him. 'Because if you are, I don't think I've finished everything I need to do.'"

Spiritual Visitation

God's answer to him was this: "No, I haven't come to take you. Don't feel badly about the things that you've been unable to accomplish. You've done the best you can with what I gave you to work with."

By that I am left to believe that God gives us each a plan and equips us with certain attributes to carry them out. His message is always to do our best, and that is all he wants us to do.

Spiritually Connected

My girlfriend and I had made plans to meet in a downtown area of a city located between us. We set the time, and independently went about our day. Later, we began getting ready to meet at our agreed upon location.

I chose the outfit to wear that evening, got dressed, and sat at the kitchen table to put on a coat of nail polish. Suddenly, I knocked the nail polish to the floor. The glass bottle broke, and red nail polish splattered all over the floor and kitchen cabinets.

I quickly got some nail polish remover and began cleaning up the mess. It took me some time, and I knew I was going to be very late. Since this was before the days of using cell phones, I was unable to contact her.

When we finally met, I explained about accidentally spilling the nail polish. She was understanding of my predicament, and we went on to enjoy the evening. It wasn't long after my explanation that she made a comment to me.

"I don't know how to tell you this," she said, "but on the way over here I could smell nail polish in my car."

The Apology

My friend, Katie, had a strained relationship with her mother for many years. While she was taking care of a sick brother, her mom's sister passed away suddenly, leaving her mom regretful for not having spoken to her for over ten years. Her stubbornness got in the way and she hurt many people.

"God sure works wondrous miracles," Katie said. "When my brother got sick, my mom apologized to my husband and I for her past behavior."

Since then, Katie and her mom repaired their wounded relationship and enjoyed many conversations together. "We connected just like we were never separated, and a healing took place for both of us.

Katie believes that with her mom losing her sister so suddenly, it made a great impact on her. She realized that she had wasted so much time and now would never get an opportunity to make that up. She also told Katie that she had a lot of healing to do with people that she had hurt over the years, including her children. She never wanted to feel that way again.

Within a few months after the apology, Katie's mom required brain surgery. The surgery resulted in a hemorrhage, which left her in a coma. Katie visited her mom in the hospital and said to her, "If you can hear me, squeeze my hand," and she did. At some point during the few weeks that she lingered on, Katie said she held her hand and thought she heard her mom say, "I'm sorry."

After some difficult weeks, Katie's mom passed on. Although she feels cheated for the years they missed together, she is grateful for the healing that took place.

The Cat Ghost

A talented singer friend of mine, Marie, does cat rescue and presently has nine cats. One night, after going to bed, she could feel a cat jump on the bed and curl up right next to her.

"It wasn't one of my cats," she said. "They had all been accounted for. Just to be sure, I checked the bedroom carefully to see if any of the cats were there, and finding none, closed the door."

Again, she could feel the cat curled up next to her, giving her warmth. When she realized it was a cat ghost, she prayed to God to please take this cat to heaven. It had obviously not crossed over.

That was the last time she felt the cat's presence. She missed having the little cat with her, so she asked God if the cat could come and visit, but still be in heaven.

The cat never returned, so she feels she got her answer. The cat could not visit her after it crossed over. She knew then that she had to let her wishful thinking go, and felt gratified that she had helped the little cat get to heaven.

The Golden Light

When I arrived home last evening, there was a message on my recorder from my friend, Marilyn, that her mother had passed away. Marilyn had never been a favorite child of her mother's, and they had spent more than fifty years trying to smooth out a bumpy relationship.

Marilyn's mom had been moved from a nursing home in Port Huron to a home in Lansing, which was more than a couple of hours away. Marilyn had taken the day before to go and visit her to find that she had just been transported from the nursing home to the hospital and was not doing well.

Despite the ill will and her mom's failing condition, she and Marilyn were able to exchange a form of peace between them at the hospital. Marilyn held her hand, and a calmness prevailed. Her mom had been happy that she was coming to visit and expressed her gladness.

The following morning, Marilyn awakened to see a golden light shine in the bedroom window onto the mirror, and reflect back out the window. She sat up in bed and looked at the light and into the mirror. She saw her own face in a light she had never seen before. She saw her face completely at peace after having had such a calming day with her mom. Shortly after, she received a call that her mom had passed on.

The Healing

I had been suffering terribly with an unknown ailment for many years. It was not recognized by doctors and therefore any medical assistance was denied. I was turned away repeatedly.

I prayed a lot for help. I prayed to St. Peter and St. Michael, the archangels. I prayed to God. I asked for relief from the torment I was enduring. No help came. At least I didn't recognize the help that I might have been getting. I tried numerous home remedies, and some very dangerous treatments, to alleviate my pain and suffering.

A little fairy visited me continuously, in my mental vision. Sometimes she would sprinkle fairy dust just prior to her visit, or I would hear a gentle little bell ringing to know that she was near. I didn't understand what her visits were all about, but she visited frequently. I expect that my praying is what caused her to come to me.

Finally, someone told me that fairies were much in favor of nature, and all things natural. After some time, I realized that she was telling me to use nature to help my condition. Going back to primitive times and cures brought me some relief, but not a cure.

As the years passed, my condition became more manageable, but I still endured much suffering. I still silently prayed for relief. Then one night as I lay sleeping soundly, a light appeared in front of my chest of drawers, waking me.

A warmth fell all over me, and Mother Mary appeared in the light. I felt that she was there to heal me. I could feel the light and heat radiate through me as I gazed at her presence. She was there for several minutes, and I soaked in the light and warmth that she brought.

I thanked her profusely, but I did not heal. I rationalized that there was only so much that she could do, and I thanked her for her valiant efforts. Much later I have come to believe that even though she wasn't able to heal my body, she surely healed my spirit. How else did I become so strong and go on living through such an ordeal? How else was I able to endure? She gave me the love and strength that I needed. That was her gift of healing.

The Little Man

I had fallen asleep on the couch for the night, and while I seldom wake up, was disturbed by something rocking my feet. I began to come out of my deep sleep. It was not uncommon for me to be disturbed by someone shaking my bed while I slept, but I never found anyone or anything there to be able to explain clearly what happened.

I could remember having been dreaming of some building which had a marquee or signboard that resembled the ivory keys of a piano. The end keys on either side were dark and perhaps a royal blue. There may have been a red or yellow key as well among them.

Now awake, with my eyes still squinted, I looked at the area near my feet to see a small little transparent man sitting there on the couch. He had obviously disturbed me when he moved my feet to sit down. He was slight of build and not a good looking man at all, but was happily mouthing a musical "da da tut tut tut" tune with his hands moving in the air.

As I opened my eyes fully, he was no longer visible. Who was he? He was light and gay—a happy little soul.

What I need to sort out is if this little man interjected the dream into my mind or if he was able to know the dream I was having. I am more apt to think that I heard his little tune and mentally placed the resemblance of piano keys on the building in my dream.

A couple of days later I had the opportunity to talk with my friend, Gwenn, and told her of this encounter with the ugly little man. I hated to call anyone ugly, but he really was not very nice looking.

"That's your Gremlin," she said. "He's there to be a brat, to make fun of you and give you a hard time. That's the ugly little man you saw."

"Really?" I could hardly believe it.

"Yes," she continued. "He will be a menace, but not really that harmful. He will want to play tricks on you. Do you know how to get rid of him?"

The Little Man

"No," I replied.

"Tell him you will tell the Blessed Mother on him. His little 'tut tut tut' tune is like 'nah nah nah nah nah nah,' so talk to Mother Mary and ask her to help you get rid of him.

"You have to change, too," she continued. "What has happened is that you have not been in very good spirits, and you have let him in. What you need to do is think only happy thoughts and not let any negativity come into your mind. Then he can't bother you."

"Well, I told you that I haven't really been interested in anything lately. I haven't been depressed, but my spirits haven't really been up either."

"That's it," Gwenn said. "You have let him in and now you will have to ask Mother Mary to help you get rid of him. He's your little Gremlin, alright!"

The Pocket Knife

Knowing that I could get information from objects, specifically metal, a friend gave me his pocket knife to see if I could give him some history of the knife.

I saw red and blue type, like type-set letters. I could hear the keying of a manual typewriter. Perhaps the knife was originally purchased through a magazine ad or some other form of advertising.

I see many, many male faces, one at a time, in great detail. The faces are live. I would judge them to be all over the age of fifty. The progression of faces is very detailed and very fast, too fast to grasp individual elements. One I remember is a gray-bearded man.

The next thing I saw was something representing heat, like hot metal. Perhaps it is a steel plant, with molten steel.

Quite strangely, I saw my Aunt Marion's face in a manufactured form, like an appliqué or a sewn patch. She was wearing the hair style that she wore in the 1960s. Then I saw her real face in living detail. I saw many screen shots of her face. Her hair was brown, a natural color. She colored it blonde in later years, a color I remember so well. I can only imagine that she was a part of the person's life who had this pocket knife at that time, but that didn't make any sense to me at all.

I then felt the impact of parts being made. I can assume the pocket knife was carried by someone working in a plant, and perhaps took part in its construction.

Next, my nose felt stuffy, and there was something packed in it. I thought about the snorting of cocaine, but that wasn't it. It's snuff, or a substance that is inhaled through the nose, I realized. It was a heavy substance and I couldn't breathe clearly. I felt it was tobacco.

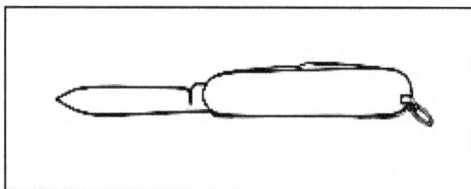

Pocket Knife

I tried to get more information during the following two nights' meditation, but that was all the information that I could get from this pocket knife.

It was some time later that I realized that my late Aunt Marion had brought me that information, and had no association with the knife or its owner. I find that she has chosen to be one of my guides as I have since seen her in my nightly visions.

The Saints Come Rolling In

I hadn't been exercising for several months, and one day found that I was getting winded with such little effort as it takes to vacuum a room. I soon got myself enrolled in an exercise class that met three times a week. I use to go to just one of the three sessions, but this time I put a concerted effort into going at least twice, finding that there was always some conflict in my schedule where I could not make all three.

I went to the first class on Monday, performing a routine of which I was quite familiar. On Wednesday, however, I had only gone to this instructor's class once before but liked her style. I found that her set of exercises involved some line dancing movements as well as a rigorous workout using weights and a stretch band. She did not let up on the execution of her routine for almost a full hour, with a customary slow down period of less than five minutes at the end.

I felt good and knew that the class had benefited me well. I had felt the use of my muscles in my thighs, but the discomfort was minor—until a couple of days later.

Oh, the pain in my body began! My left side hurt from my butt and down my leg, right to the ankle. I thought I was feeling sciatic nerve damage, but found it was only from the exertion of muscles I hadn't used in a while. I began to wrap the parts that hurt with whatever elastic bandages and braces I could find. I couldn't get comfortable in bed, and therefore could not sleep.

I finally settled into a melancholy state, when I could sense a couple of visual rolling balls of some substance coming toward me quite rapidly. I waited, and found that St. Michael arrived first with his bright yellow light, immediately followed by St. Germain in his violet cast of color. I had learned that they often traveled together.

I was so accustomed to their visits, that I greeted them this way: "Oh, hi guys!" I feel that they are my friends with their caring interruptions to my solitude. No words transpired, and their visit ended shortly after their arrival. I assume that they knew I was in pain, and had come to comfort me and be by my side. They wanted to let me know that they were aware of my condition.   I thanked them, and could only think of these words: "When the Saints Come Rolling In."

The Spiritual Rug

My husband lost his previous wife a year before we met. I learned that she was a religious person, as was he, and both were very spiritual. In fact, of the many things that I learned about her, she was so intent in her prayers that she healed her terminally ill sister.

Among her many interests, she loved angels and Christmas, and fervently celebrated the birth of the Lord. While I don't display such an outward admiration, my own talents of spiritual connection with Jesus present a comfort to my husband.

When we married, we discussed that his previous wife must have played a part in bringing us together. He felt that she had directed him to me. I confirmed that I had received a Tarot card reading indicating that I would meet a man who fit his spiritual description, and that I did in fact meet him in the timing stated by the reader.

For months after our meeting, I felt that the previous wife was trying to communicate with me by the frequent vibrations that I experienced in my ear. I had no comprehension of what she was trying to say, and in time, the interruptions became annoying. I wished they would stop, and they finally did.

This year new furniture and an area rug were purchased for our living room. While shopping, my husband picked out the rug that matched the furniture well, and I liked it very much. It had been home on the floor for some time when I noticed some distinguishing things in the rug's subtle design. Not only did it have spiritual doves and flowers in the background, there were angels above shapes like Christmas trees.

The finding and purchase of this rug was obviously not by accident. It was meant to be a reminder of her influence in our relationship and the continuing interest of God and spirituality in our lives.

The Violet Flame

For the last few years, I have experienced seeing a mind's eye vision of a bluish purple and yellow light. From some misgivings, I thought it was St. Michael, the Archangel, and that he was present.

Then one day I sought out a new card reader. I found that she had a great connection with angels, and she read from several decks of cards, none of which were familiar to me.

In my discussion with her, I mentioned the vision that I thought was St. Michael, and that he visited quite frequently. After hearing what I described, she thought that maybe I was seeing the Violet Flame, brought by St. Germain.

I had researched the Violet Flame previously, but did not identify it to what I was seeing. The pictures that I found showed a bluish purple with a yellow center, and what I saw had the yellow as a border around a bluish purple center. The next time I saw the reader, she again suggested that I was seeing the Violet Flame.

This time she told me that I should concentrate more on myself if I was to succeed in the endeavors that I wanted to accomplish. She said that I spent too much of my time trying to help others.

After researching the Violet Flame again, I have now accepted that the light that I see is actually the Violet Flame, and that St. Michael often accompanies St. Germain. That is why the yellow light appears first, and then St. Germain's Violet Flame follows.

I have also learned that there are mantras and decrees that should be said in order to access the power of the Violet Flame.

This power can be used to help others, and the entire universe. That leaves me with a dilemma of wanting to use it to help others, or wondering if I should follow the advice of my reader to help myself first.

There is a Heaven

Marsha, my musically inclined friend, has a very busy mind. She questions everything, but especially those spiritual things she does not understand. She is very much in touch with God, but still, she questions.

"When my father passed on, I really wanted to know if he was in heaven. Is there really a heaven?" she kept asking in prayer. Not getting a formal answer, she sought out a psychic reader.

The reader could see her father in heaven, and told her so, as well as other things about him that confirmed that her words were true.

Months later, thinking about her late mother, she again sought out this same reader. "Is my mother in heaven too?" she queried.

The reader again confirmed her mother's presence in heaven. "Your mother loved flowers," she said. "She is truly enjoying the many flowers of heaven as their colors are so vibrant and they are different than the flowers around here."

Now Marsha says she knows there is a heaven, and is at peace for her parents.

Time Warp

Some years ago, while shopping with some friends in a nearby city, I found myself in a sudden time warp. My steps were caught in a freeze frame, and I seemed to remain there for several seconds. I also seem to recall a surreal sound in my head as I was frozen in space and time.

I had been told by a card reader that a deceased person would be trying to contact me, and other elements during my shopping day confirmed that he indeed was near.

I was talking on the telephone with my daughter recently. I was on a landline, and she was using her cell phone. I had just posed a question to her, and the line appeared to have gone dead.

I punched a couple of buttons, trying to find out if I had lost the call when, about five seconds later, her answer suddenly came through as if there was no gap in time at all.

She continued with her little chatter until I interrupted her to ask this question. "Did you notice a break in our conversation a few minutes ago where the line went dead?"

"No, I didn't," she replied, but it makes me wonder what really went on. Was that interruption from that same deceased person several years later? He was more connected to my daughter than to me, and maybe he was letting me know that he was around.

Travel to Egypt

Jill, a dear friend of mine who likes to travel, took a trip to Egypt. While there, she had a totally phenomenal encounter. She toured the Luxor Temple and saw the many statues.

As a total surprise to her, she began to cry profusely when she found that her late mother was talking to her through one of the statues. She could not understand what was being said, but it was a totally emotional and astonishing experience.

I asked one of my psychic gentleman acquaintances what he thought about this. He felt that this was probably not the first communication that the mother had tried to make with her, and that it probably had something to do with one or more incarnations.

Up, Down, and Around

All day long I had asked the spirit world for answers to a given situation in my life. I did not receive an answer until I was awakened at 3:00 a.m. by a vibration in my left ear.

A little fairy, whom I have named Tinker Bell, tried to make me understand. I was shown a completely round, natural colored basket that had no handles. It had pink ribbon woven in and out of the basket. I asked her to please give me words, as I did not understand what this meant.

Then I sensed a male trying to assist me. I called him Peter, after Peter Pan, as he had come with Tinker Bell. He showed me a home cooling fan that was lying down, and I could see fan blades moving up, down, and around.

Again I asked for words as I was at a loss. Instead, I heard the words from the song, "Upside Down." It was sung by Diana Ross, and the words I heard were "inside out, the way you turn me," which I believe was popular around the late 1990s.

Finally, I sensed the word "forgiveness." Perhaps this was because I could not hear any words and still did not understand. Perhaps they were letting me know that they were sorry.

Then, my last visual was presented. I saw a twirling skirt, and the fabric of the skirt was moving up, down and around.

I told all of the information to my friend, Gwenn, who has assisted me with many of my visual encounters. She said, "That's just what you've been doing, going up, down, and around, trying to find a solution to your problem.

Vertigo

The last couple of years I have had an ailment called positional vertigo. It is not bothersome at all in a sitting or standing position, but when I lay down, there is one position that produces "room spins."

At first I was quite worried and went to the doctor and received that diagnosis. After explaining that I was afraid I had a brain tumor, I was sent for an MRI to be sure that I did not have one.

The other evening, after lying down in bed, I was presented with spiritual images in my mind's eye. Strangely, the visions were presented slightly slanted. "That's weird," I exclaimed, and went to sleep.

A couple of nights later, another image was presented, and as I began to concentrate on the details, it began to spin! "Okay," I said to the spirit world. "So you know I have vertigo. Very funny!"

Voices

I was home alone, busily doing chores around the house, when I heard my husband's voice announcing that he was home. Or at least I thought I heard him call me when he walked in the door, but he was not there. Who did I hear, I wondered?

Another time, while sleeping, I was awakened to hear voices in the house. I picked my head up off the pillow, and could still hear them.

I got out of bed and walked through the kitchen. I thought maybe my husband had forgotten to turn off the television in the living room before going to bed. I checked, but it was off. So was the radio in his office. No one was in the house.

I checked outside the house, and all around, to see if someone was outside at either next-door neighbor, but found no one. There was no sign of anyone.

I wondered, did I just hear angels or my guides talking? Did they not realize that I could hear them?

Wake Up

"Ellen, are you awake?" I heard. I was then, but I didn't want to wake up. I patted my husband on the shoulder and turned over to go back to sleep.

Later, when we were having coffee, I asked him if he tried to wake me earlier. "No," he said.

"Well, someone asked me if I was awake, and I patted you on the shoulder to let you know I heard, but didn't want to wake up."

"I remember you patting me, but I didn't talk to you. That must have been one of your guides."

"I wonder why they wanted me to wake up."

Watching Over Him

I've commented on my Money Angel numerous times and now find that she has clearly taken it upon herself to watch over my husband as well. He not only finds more change on the ground than I do, she has come to present him with things that he has wished for just as she does for me.

He has a windsock in the backyard. He watches it daily to detect wind direction, but it has become tattered and torn from recent storms. "If you see a better windsock somewhere, pick it up for me," he requested.

He also remarked to me several times, "If you go to a garage sale and see those ceramic fireplace logs, buy them." He wanted to add logs to our gas fireplace. My thoughts were: I'm not buying them, should I happen to see any, which is highly unlikely.

Well, I never seem to have the time to stop at garage sales, but one day my husband and I were out, and we stopped at an estate sale. I find it very strange that he found a good quality windsock, as well as those fireplace logs that he has been wanting.

When in Texas

I was getting ready to go out, and my mind mentally went to a time that I had worked in Texas. A word came to me psychically: "Pleblano." I was clear about the spelling.

Much of the food in Texas is Mexican, and a fair amount contains their chili peppers, called poblano. I did some research, and my spelling "pleblano" was corrected to be "poblano."

However, as I dug deeper, I found my spelling in what I think was an older Spanish document.

Do I have a Spanish guide that gave me that word?

You Should Rest

I had just spent a hectic day running from place to place to do errands. Just doing the grocery shopping had tired me out, but I pressed on to finish everything that I needed to do.

When I returned home and put all of the groceries away, I took a few minutes to sit down in a chair and relax. Just then, a flash vision crossed my internal sight, and I saw Jesus laying down, flat on his back, with his arms folded across his chest.

"You should rest," was the infused message that I got from that vision. Jesus was telling me that I should rest!

Books by Ellen Marie Blend

Books of Psychic Phenomena

Visual Encounters

Unraveling The Weave

Looking Back

Conversing on a Higher Level

Impunity from Lunacy – Book One

An Autobiography

Not About Money
(A Career story: downsizing and discrimination)

A Biography

The Educator
(The Teaching Skills of Bernard F. Nanni)